Poetry

£2.50

31

D1436674

5
46.

THE VOYAGE

ALSO BY EDWIN MUIR

*

THE NARROW PLACE

THE VOYAGE AND
OTHER POEMS

BY

EDWIN MUIR

FABER AND FABER
LONDON

To
LUMIR and CATRIONA

First published in Mcmxlvi
by Faber and Faber Limited
24 Russell Square London, W.C.1.
Printed in Great Britain by
R. MacLehose and Company Limited
The University Press Glasgow
All rights reserved

CONTENTS

6

THE RETURN

The veteran Greeks came home
Sleepwandering from the war.
We saw the galleys come
Blundering over the bar.
Each soldier with his scar
In rags and tatters came home.

Reading the wall of Troy
Ten years without a change
Was such intense employ
(Just out of the arrows' range),
All the world was strange
After ten years of Troy.

Their eyes knew every stone
In the huge heartbreaking wall
Year after year grown
Till there was nothing at all
But an alley steep and small,
Tramped earth and towering stone.

Now even the hills seemed low
In the boundless sea and land,
Weakened by distance so.
How could they understand
Space empty on every hand
And the hillocks squat and low?

And when they arrived at last
They found a childish scene
Embosomed in the past,
And the war lying between—
A child's preoccupied scene
When they came home at last.

7

But everything trite and strange,
The peace, the parcelled ground,
The vinerows—never a change!
The past and the present bound
In one oblivious round
Past thinking trite and strange.

But for their grey-haired wives
And their sons grown shy and tall
They would have given their lives
To raise the battered wall
Again, if this was all
In spite of their sons and wives.

Penelope in her tower
Looked down upon the show
And saw within an hour
Each man to his wife go,
Hesitant, sure and slow:
She, alone in her tower.

THE ESCAPE

Escaping from the enemy's hand
    Into the enemy's vast domain,
I sought by many a devious path,
    Having got in, to get out again.

The endless trap lay everywhere,
    And all the roads ran in a maze
Hither and thither, like a web
    To catch the careless days.

The great farmhouses sunk in time
    Rose up out of another land;
Here only the empty harvest-home
    Where Caliban waved his wand.

There was no promise in the bud,
    No comfort in the blossoming tree,
The waving yellow harvests were
    Worse than sterility.

Yet all seemed true. The family group
    Still gathered round the dying hearth,
The old men droned the ancient saws,
    And the young mother still gave birth.

But this I saw there. In the church
    In rows the stabled horses stood,
And the cottar's threshold stone
    Was mired with earth and blood.

And when I reached the line between
    The Occupied and Unoccupied,
It was as hard as death to cross,
    Yet no change on the other side.

All false, all one. The enemy
    These days was scarcely visible;
Only his work was everywhere,
    Ill work contrived so well

That he could smile and turn his back,
  Let brute indifference overawe
The longing flesh and leaping heart
  And grind to dust the ancient law.

A land of bright delusion where
  Shape scarce disturbed the emptiness
Yet troubled the sight that strove to make
  Of every shape a shape the less.

There the perpetual question ran,
  What is escape? and What is flight?
Like dialogue in a dismal dream
  Where right is wrong and wrong is right.

But at the very frontier line,
  Beyond the region of desire,
There runs a wall of towering flame:
  The battle is there of blood and fire.

I must pass through that fiery wall,
  Emerge into the battle place,
And there at last, lifting my eyes,
  I'll see the enemy's face.

THE CASTLE

All through that summer at ease we lay,
And daily from the turret wall
We watched the mowers in the hay
And the enemy half a mile away.
They seemed no threat to us at all.

For what, we thought, had we to fear
With our arms and provender, load on load,
Our towering battlements, tier on tier,
And friendly allies drawing near
On every leafy summer road.

Our gates were strong, our walls were thick,
So smooth and high, no man could win
A foothold there, no clever trick
Could take us, have us dead or quick.
Only a bird could have got in.

What could they offer us for bait?
Our captain was brave and we were true . . .
There was a little private gate,
A little wicked wicket gate.
The wizened warder let them through.

Oh then our maze of tunnelled stone
Grew thin and treacherous as air.
The cause was lost without a groan,
The famous citadel overthrown,
And all its secret galleries bare.

How can this shameful tale be told?
I will maintain until my death
We could do nothing, being sold;
Our only enemy was gold,
And we had no arms to fight it with.

MOSES

He left us there, went up to Pisgah hill,
And saw the holiday land, the sabbath land,
The mild prophetic beasts, millennial herds,
The sacred lintel, over-arching tree,
The vineyards glittering on the southern slopes,
And in the midst the shining vein of water,
The river turning, turning towards its home.
Promised to us. The dream rose in his nostrils
With homely smell of wine and corn and cattle,
Byre, barn and stall, sweat-sanctified smell of peace.
He saw the tribes arrayed beside the river,
White robes and sabbath stillness, still light falling
On dark heads whitened by the desert wave,
The Sabbath of Sabbaths come and Canaan their home.
All this he saw in dreaming. But we who dream
Such common dreams and see so little saw
The battle for the land, the massacres,
The vineyards drenched in aboriginal blood,
The settlement, unsatisfactory order,
The petty wars and neighbouring jealousies
And local troubles. But we did not see,
We did not see and Moses did not see,
The great disaster, exile, diaspora,
The holy bread of the land crumbled and broken
In Babylon, Caesarea, Alexandria
As on a splendid dish, or gnawed as offal.
Nor did we see, beyond, the ghetto rising,
Toledo, Cracow, Vienna, Budapesth,
Nor, had we seen, would we have known our people
In the wild disguises of fantastic time,
Packed in dense cities, wandering countless roads,
And not a road in the world to lead them home.
How could we have seen such things? How could we have
    seen

That plot of ground pledged by the God of Moses
Trampled by sequent tribes, seized and forgotten
As a child seizes and forgets a toy,
Strange languages, strange gods and customs borne
Over it and away with the light migrations,
Stirring each century ancestral dust.
All this was settled while we stood by Jordan
That first great day, could not be otherwise.
Moses saw that day only; we did not see it;
But now it stands becalmed in time for ever:
White robes and sabbath peace, the snow-white emblem.

SAPPHO

Sappho, Sappho's pitiless murderess,
Strides in judgment through the end of night
To circumvent the round blue trap of day
(That soon will lock its jail of miseries),
Drives her victim to the penal rock,
Angry, abrupt, broken-off edge of time.
Pursuer and pursued
Tied each to each by such a sullen knot
No arrowy thought of immaterial god
Can slip between and ease the torment crying:
'All my life cries out against all my life,
My love against all my love. I'll carry Phaon
Until I drop or leap the final crag
Where all is left behind, things and their names.
For if a single name should follow there
I must reiterate this death and leap
Precipice after precipice of death
Till name of wood and hill and night and day
And all that summons Phaon is stripped off.'

Now the dumb hulks of being rise around her:
Beast, rock and tree, illegible figures, stare
At her in destitution as on the day
Before the first day broke, when all was nameless,
Nameless earth, water, firmament, and nameless
Woman and man. Till on the utmost edge
She leans above the unanswering shapes of life,
Cries once and leaps, and battered on the stones,
Batters love, Phaon and all the misery out.

THE COVENANT

The covenant of god and animal,
The frieze of fabulous creatures winged and crowned,
And in the midst the woman and the man—

Lost long ago in fields beyond the Fall—
Keep faith in sleep-walled night and there are found
On our long journey back where we began.

Then the heraldic crest of nature lost
Shines out again until the weariless wave
Roofs with its sliding horror all that realm.

What jealousy, what rage could overwhelm
The golden lion and lamb and vault a grave
For innocence, innocence past defence or cost?

THOUGHT AND IMAGE

Past time and space the shaping Thought
   Was born in freedom and in play;
The Image then on earth was wrought
   Of water and of clay.

And when the embodied Soul would know
   Itself and be to itself revealed,
For its instruction it must go
   To the beast that roams the field.

Thenceforth the Soul grew intimate
   With beast and herb and stone, and passed
Into the elements to mate
   With the dull earth at last.

It's said that to reverse its doom
   And save the entangled Soul, to earth
God came and entered in the womb
   And passed through the gate of birth;

Was born a Child in body bound
   Among the cattle in a byre.
The clamorous world was all around,
   Beast, insect, plant, earth, water, fire.

On bread and wine his flesh grew tall,
   The round sun helped him on his way,
Wood, iron, herb and animal
   His friends were till the testing day.

Then braced by iron and by wood,
   Engrafted on a tree he died,
And little dogs lapped up the blood
   That spurted from his broken side.

The great bull gored him with his horns,
    And stinging flies were everywhere,
The sun beat on him, winding thorns
    Writhed in and out among his hair.

His body next was locked in stone,
    By steel preserved in sterile trust,
And with the earth was left alone,
    And, dust, lay with the dust.

There all at last with all was done,
    The great knot loosened, flesh unmade
Beyond the kingdom of the sun,
    In the invincible shade.

All that had waited for his birth
    Were round him then in dusty night,
The creatures of the swarming earth,
    The souls and angels in the height.

TWICE-DONE, ONCE-DONE

Nothing yet was ever done
  Till it was done again,
And no man was ever one
  Except through dead men.

I could neither rise nor fall
  But that Adam fell.
Had he fallen once for all
  There'd be nothing to tell.

Unless in me my fathers live
  I can never show
I am myself—ignorant if
  I'm a ghost or no.

Father Adam and Mother Eve,
  Make this pact with me:
Teach me, teach me to believe,
  For to believe's to be.

Many a woman since Eve was made
  Has seen the world is young,
Many and many a time obeyed
  The legend-making tongue.

Abolish the ancient custom—who
  Would mark Eve on her shelf?
Even a story to be true
  Must repeat itself.

Yet we the latest born are still
  The first ones and the last,
And in our little measures fill
  The oceanic past.

For first and last is every way,
  And first and last each soul,
And first and last the passing day,
  And first and last the goal.

DIALOGUE

'Now let us lover by lover lay
   And enemy now to enemy bring,
Set open the immaculate way
   Of everything to everything
   And crown our destiny king.'

'If lover were by lover laid,
   And enemy brought to enemy,
All that's made would be unmade
   And done would be the destiny
   Of time and eternity.

'But love with love can never rest,
   And hate can never bear with hate,
Each by each must be possessed,
   For, see, at every turning wait
   The enemy and the mate.'

THE VOYAGE

(For Eric Linklater)

That sea was greater than we knew.
Week after week the empty round
Went with us; the Unchanging grew,
And we were headed for that bound.

How we came there we could not tell.
Seven storms had piled us in that peace,
Put us in check and barred us well
With seven walls of seven seas.

As one may vanish in a day
In some untravelled fold of space
And there pursue his patient way
Yet never come to any place

Though following still by star and sun,
For every chart is rased and furled,
And he out of this world has run
And wanders now another world,

So we by line and compass steered
And conned the book of sun and star,
Yet where it should no sign appeared
To tell us, You are there or there,

Familiar landfall, slender mast:
We on the ocean were alone.
The busy lanes where fleets had passed
Showed us no sail except our own.

Still south we steered day after day
And only water lay around
As if the land had stolen away
Or sprawled upon the ocean ground.

The sun by day, the stars by night
Had only us to look upon,
Bent on us their collected light,
And followed on as we went on.

Sometimes in utter wonder lost
That loneliness like this could be
We stood and stared until almost
We saw no longer sky or sea,

But only the frame of time and space,
An empty floor, a vacant wall,
And on that blank no line to trace
Movement, if we moved at all.

What thoughts came then! Sometimes it seemed
We long had passed the living by
On other seas and only dreamed
This sea, this journey and this sky,

Or traced a ghostly parallel
That limned the land but could not merge,
And haven and home and harbour bell
Were just behind the horizon verge,

Or the world itself had ended so
Without a cry, and we should sail
To and fro, to and fro,
Long past the lightning and the gale.

O then what crowding fantasies
Poured in from empty sea and sky!
At night we heard the whispering quays,
Line after line, slide softly by.

Delusions in the silent noon;
Fields in the hollows of the waves;
Or spread beneath the yellow moon,
A land of harvests and of graves.

The soft sea-sounds beguiled our ear.
We thought we walked by mountain rills
Or listened half a night to hear
The spring wind hunting on the hills.

And faces, faces, faces came
Across the salt sea-desert air,
And rooms in which a candle flame
Made everything renowned and rare.

The words we knew like our right hand,
Mountain and valley, meadow and grove,
Composed a legendary land
Rich with the broken tombs of love.

Delusion or truth? We were content
Thenceforth to sail the harmless seas
Safe past the Fate and the Accident,
And called a blessing on that peace.

And blessing, we ourselves were blest,
Lauded the loss that brought our gain,
Sang the tumultuous world to rest,
And wishless called it back again.

For loss was then our only joy,
Privation of all, fulfilled desire,
The world our treasure and our toy
In destitution clean as fire.

Our days were then—I cannot tell
How we were then fulfilled and crowned
With life as in a parable,
And sweetly as gods together bound.

Delusion and dream! Our captain knew
Compass and clock had never yet
Failed him; the sun and stars were true.
The mark was there that we should hit.

And it rose up, a sullen stain
Flawing the crystal firmament.
A wound! We felt the familiar pain
And knew the place to which we were sent.

The crowds drew near, the toppling towers;
In hope and dread we drove to birth;
The dream and a truth we clutched as ours,
And gladly, blindly stepped on earth.

THE FATHERS

Our fathers all were poor,
Poorer our fathers' fathers;
Beyond, we dare not look.
We, the sons, keep store
Of tarnished gold that gathers
Around us from the night,
Record it in this book
That, when the line is drawn,
Credit and creditor gone,
Column and figure flown,
Will open into light.

Archaic fevers shake
Our healthy flesh and blood
Plumped in the passing day
And fed with pleasant food.
The fathers' anger and ache
Will not, will not away
And leave the living alone,
But on our careless brows
Faintly their furrows engrave
Like veinings in a stone,
Breathe in the sunny house
Nightmare of blackened bone,
Cellar and choking cave.

Panics and furies fly
Through our unhurried veins,
Heavenly lights and rains
Purify heart and eye,
Past agonies purify
And lay the sullen dust.

The angers will not away.
We hold our fathers' trust,
Wrong, riches, sorrow and all
Until they topple and fall,
And fallen let in the day.

THE THREE MIRRORS

I looked in the first glass
And saw the fenceless field
And like broken stones in grass
The sad towns glint and shine.
The slowly twisting vine
Scribbled with wrath the stone,
The mountain summits were sealed
In incomprehensible wrath.
The hunting roads ran on
To round the flying hill
And bring the quarry home.
But the obstinate roots ran wrong,
The lumbering fate fell wrong,
The walls were askew with ill,
Askew went every path,
The dead lay askew in the tomb.

I looked in the second glass
And saw through the twisted scroll
In virtue undefiled
And new in eternity
Father and mother and child,
The house with its single tree,
Bed and board and cross,
And the dead asleep in the knoll.
But the little blade and leaf
By an angry law were bent
To shapes of terror and grief,
By a law the field was rent,
The crack ran over the floor,
The child at peace in his play
Changed as he passed through a door,
Changed were the house and the tree,
Changed the dead in the knoll,

For locked in love and grief
Good with evil lay.

If I looked in the third glass
I should see evil and good
Standing side by side
In the ever standing wood,
The wise king safe on his throne,
The rebel raising the rout,
And each so deeply grown
Into his own place
He'd be past desire or doubt.
If I could look I should see
The world's house open wide,
The million million rooms
And the quick god everywhere
Glowing at work and at rest,
Tranquillity in the air,
Peace of the humming looms
Weaving from east to west,
And you and myself there.

THE RIDER VICTORY

The rider Victory reins his horse
Midway across the empty bridge
As if head-tall he had met a wall.
Yet there was nothing there at all,
No bodiless barrier, ghostly ridge
To check the charger in his course
So suddenly, you'd think he'd fall.

Suspended, horse and rider stare,
Leaping on air and legendary.
In front the waiting kingdom lies,
The bridge and all the roads are free;
But halted in implacable air
Rider and horse with stony eyes
Uprear their motionless statuary.

THE WINDOW

Within the great wall's perfect round
Bird, beast and child serenely grew
In endless change on changeless ground
That in a single pattern bound
The old perfection and the new.

There was a tower set in the wall
And a great window in the tower,
And if one looked, beyond recall
The twisting glass kept him in thrall
With changing marvels hour by hour.
And there one day we looked and saw
Marsh, mere and mount in anger shaken,
The world's great side, the giant flaw,
And watched the stately forests fall,
The white ships sinking in the sea,
The tower run toppling in the field,
The last left stronghold sacked and taken,
And earth and heaven in jeopardy.
Then turning towards you I beheld
The wrinkle writhe across your brow,
And felt Time's cap clapped on my head,
And all within the enclosure now,
Light leaf and smiling flower, was false,
The great wall breached, the garden dead.

Across the towering window fled
Disasters, victories, festivals.

THE HOUSE

The young and the lusty loll in bed
And the bent and the aged lay the fire
And sweep the floor and cook the food.
'No reason or rule is in this house,'

Sighed the little old woman, shaking her head,
'Where the young and the rich have their desire,
And all the reward of the poor and the good
Is to prop the walls of this thankless house.

'Yes', she muttered, '*they*'ve all they want,
But we have nothing but knowledge to chew,
Only that, and necessity.
These two maintain this niggardly house.

'For the young and the rich are ignorant
And never guess what they've yet to rue—
The lenten days when they will be
Servants like us of this tyrannous house.'

THE MYTH

My childhood all a myth
Enacted in a distant isle;
Time with his hourglass and his scythe
Stood dreaming on the dial,
And did not move the whole day long
That immobility might save
Continually the dying song,
The flower, the falling wave.
And at each corner of the wood
In which I played the ancient play,
Guarding the traditional day
The faithful watchers stood.

My youth a tragi-comedy,
Ridiculous war of dreams and shames
Waged for a Pyrrhic victory
Of reveries and names,
Which in slow-motion rout were hurled
Before sure-footed flesh and blood
That of its hunger built a world,
Advancing rood by rood.
And there in practical clay compressed
The reverie played its useful part,
Fashioning a diurnal mart
Of radiant east and west.

So manhood went. Now past the prime
I see this life contrived to stay
With all its works of labouring time
By time beguiled away.
Consolidated flesh and bone
And its designs grow halt and lame;
Unshakeable arise alone
The reverie and the name.

And at each border of the land,
Like monuments a deluge leaves,
Guarding the invisible sheaves
The risen watchers stand.

ON SEEING TWO LOVERS IN
THE STREET

You do not know
What is done with you,
Do not fear
What's done or undone:
You are not here,
You are not two
Any more, but one.

Pity these two
Who all have lost,
Envy these two
Who have paid their cost
To gain this soul
That dazzling hovered
Between them whole.
There they are lost
And their tracks are covered;
Nothing can find them
Until they awake
In themselves or take
New selves to bind them.

SONG

Why should your face so please me
That if one little line should stray
Bewilderment would seize me
And drag me down the tortuous way
Out of the noon into the night?
But so, into this tranquil light
You raise me.

How could our minds so marry
That, separate, blunder to and fro,
Make for a point, miscarry,
And blind as headstrong horses go?
Though now they in their promised land
At pleasure travel hand in hand
Or tarry.

This concord is an answer
To questions far beyond our mind
Whose image is a dancer.
All effort is to ease refined
Here, weight is light; this is the dove
Of love and peace, not heartless love
The lancer.

And yet I still must wonder
That such an armistice can be
And life roll by in thunder
To leave this calm with you and me.
This tranquil voice of silence, yes,
This single song of two, this is
A wonder.

SUBURBAN DREAM

Walking the suburbs in the afternoon
In summer when the idle doors stand open
   And the air flows through the rooms
   Fanning the curtain hems,

You wander through a cool elysium
Of women, schoolgirls, children, garden talks,
   With a schoolboy here and there
   Conning his history book.

The men are all away in offices,
Committee-rooms, laboratories, banks,
   Or pushing cotton goods
   In Wick or Ilfracombe.

The massed unanimous absence liberates
The light keys of the piano and sets free
   Chopin and everlasting youth,
   Now, with the masters gone.

And all things turn to images of peace,
The boy curled over his book, the young girl poised
   On the path as if beguiled
   By the silence of a wood.

It is a child's dream of a grown-up world.
But soon the brazen evening clocks will bring
   The tramp of feet and brisk
   Fanfare of motor horns
   And the masters come.

READING IN WARTIME

Boswell by my bed,
Tolstoy on my table:
Though the world has bled
For four and a half years,
And wives' and mothers' tears
Collected would be able
To water a little field
Untouched by anger and blood,
A penitential yield
Somewhere in the world;
Though in each latitude
Armies like forests fall,
The iniquitous and the good
Head over heels hurled,
And confusion over all:
Boswell's turbulent friend
And his deafening verbal strife,
Ivan Ilych's death
Tell me more about life,
The meaning and the end
Of our familiar breath,
Both being personal,
Than all the carnage can,
Retrieve the shape of man,
Lost and anonymous,
Tell me wherever I look
That not one soul can die
Of this or any clan
Who is not one of us
And has a personal tie
Perhaps to someone now
Searching an ancient book,
Folk-tale or country song
In many and many a tongue,

To find the original face,
The individual soul,
The eye, the lip, the brow
For ever gone from their place,
And gather an image whole.

THE LULLABY

The lullaby has crooned to sleep so many
On all the iron fields in such a clamour,
    There is astonishment
    Among the waking.

So quickly these awake were cast in slumber,
Full in the light, then covered thick in shadow,
    There seemed no time to shed
    Them from the others.

So deafening the clamour, soft the crooning,
So swift the change and simple the confusion,
    That these though side by side
    Were far asunder.

The returning and the unreturning races,
Those who took heed, and those who would not listen
    But turned straight towards the dark,
    So that there was nothing

To do or say, no greeting on their journey,
Farewell or words at all—these two are haunted
    For ever each by each,
    In each commingled.

DEJECTION

I do not want to be
Here, there or anywhere;
My melancholy
Folds me beyond the reach of care
As in a valley
Whence long ago I tried to sally,
But dreamt and left my dream upon the air.

And now in lunar pleasure
I watch the undreaming folk of rock and stone
Lie side by side alone
Enjoying their enormous leisure,
That shall continue till the day
When rock and stone are put away;
And feel no more than they the sun that burns
On this unmoving scenery,
Nor count nor care to count the dull returns
Of day and month and year and century
Crowding within the crowding urns.

For every eloquent voice dies in this air
Wafted from anywhere to anywhere
And never counted by the careful clock,
That cannot strike the hour
Of power that will dissolve this power
Until the rock rise up and split the rock.

SONG OF PATIENCE

What use has patience,
Won with such difficulty,
Forced out in such a sigh?

The heart in its stations
Has need of patience,
Holding through night and day
Solitary monologue,
Systole and diastole,
Two surly words that say
Each to each in the breast:
'Solid flesh, fluttering soul,
Troubles and fears, troubles and fears,
Quick hope, long delay,
Where is rest? Where is rest?'
Prologue and epilogue
Reiterated in the breast
For thirty, forty, fifty years.
The heart in its stations
Has need of patience.

Patience wearies of itself,
Impatient patience,
For itself can find no use
But to rehearse upon the shelf
Its hackneyed stations,
And so would end the long abuse,
Make each breath its parting breath,
Die in pain, be born in pain,
And to love at last attain:
Love to whom all things are well,
Love that turns all things to ease,
The life that fleets before the eye,
And the motionless isle of death;

That tunes the tedious miseries
And even patience makes to please;
Love to whom the sorrows tell
Their abysmal dreams and cry:
'Weave the spell! Weave the spell!
Make us well.'

SONG

Here in this corner
Deep in the morning,
Here you will stay.

Here is the warner,
Here the warning
And here the way.

Light here is dark;
Light be your work,
And light your play.

Brightness to wrap you in,
Darkness to lap you in,
No farewell to say,
You cannot away.

Keep fast your mystery;
Time has no history,
All things are clear,
Fear not your fear,
You cannot away.

Then wrap you and lap you within the long day,
And drop no tear
For the star or the sphere,
There's no anywhere
But here, but here.

SORROW

I do not want it so,
But since things so are made,
Sorrow, sorrow,
Be you my second trade.
I'll learn the workman's skill
And mould the mass of ill
Until I have it so, or so,
And want it so.

I cannot have it so
Unless I frankly make
A pact with sorrow
For joy and sorrow's sake,
And wring from sorrow's pay
Wealth joy would toss away—
Till both are balanced, so, or so,
And even go.

If it were only so . . .
But right and left I find
Sorrow, sorrow,
And cannot be resigned,
Knowing that we were made
By joy to drive joy's trade
And not to waver to and fro,
But quickly go.

EPITAPH

Into the grave, into the grave with him.
Quick, quick, with dust and stones this dead man cover
Who living was a flickering soul so dim
He was never truly loved nor truly a lover.

Since he was half and half, now let him be
Something entire at last here in this night
Which teaches us its absolute honesty
Who stray between the light and the half-light.

He scarce had room for sorrow, even his own;
His vastest dreams were less than six feet tall;
Free of all joys, he crept in himself alone:
To the grave with this poor image of us all.

If now is Resurrection, then let stay
Only what's ours when this is put away.

COMFORT IN SELF-DESPITE

When in revulsion I detest myself
Thus heartily, myself with myself appal,
And in this mortal rubbish delve and delve,
A dustman damned—perhaps the original

Virtue I'd thought so snugly buried so
May yet be found, else never to be found,
And thus exhumed into the light may grow
After this cruel harrowing of the ground.

For as when I have spoken spitefully
Of this or that friend, piling ill on ill,
Remembrance cleans his image and I see
The pure and touching good no taunt could kill,

So I may yet recover by this bad
Research that good I scarcely dreamt I had.

THE TRANSMUTATION

That all should change to ghost and glance and gleam,
And so transmuted stand beyond all change,
And we be poised between the unmoving dream
And the sole moving moment—this is strange

Past all contrivance, word, or image, or sound,
Or silence, to express, that we who fall
Through Time's long ruin should weave this phantom ground
And in its ghostly borders gather all.

There incorruptible the child plays still,
The lover waits beside the trysting tree,
The good hour spans its heaven, and the ill,
Rapt in their silent immortality,

As in commemoration of a day
That having been can never pass away.

TIME HELD IN TIME'S DESPITE

Now there is only left what Time has made
Our very own in our and Time's despite,
And we ourselves have nothing, but are stayed
By lonely joys and griefs and blank delight.

For this that's ours so surely could not be
But by the word of terror or of grace
That spoke, when all was lost, the guarantee:
'Impersonally soul and soul embrace,

And incorruptibly are bodies bound.'
The hours that melt like snowflakes one by one
Leave us this residue, this virgin ground
For ever fresh, this firmament and this sun.

Then let us lay unasking hand in hand,
And take our way, thus led, into our land.

TO ANN SCOTT-MONCRIEFF
(1914-1943)

Dear Ann, wherever you are
Since you lately learnt to die,
You are this unsetting star
That shines unchanged in my eye;
So near, inaccessible,
Absent and present so much
Since out of the world you fell,
Fell from hearing and touch—
So near. But your mortal tongue
Used for immortal use,
The grace of a woman young,
The air of an early muse,
The wealth of the chambered brow
And soaring flight of your eyes:
These are no longer now.
Death has a princely prize.

You who were Ann much more
Then others are that or this,
Extravagant over the score
To be what only is,
Would you not still say now
What you once used to say
Of the great Why and How,
On that or the other day?
For though of your heritage
The minority here began,
Now you have come of age
And are entirely Ann.

Under the years' assaults,
In the storm of good and bad,
You too had the faults
That Emily Brontë had,

Ills of body and soul,
Of sinner and saint and all
Who strive to make themselves whole,
Smashed to bits by the Fall.
Yet 'the world is a pleasant place'
I can hear your voice repeat,
While the sun shone in your face
Last summer in Princes Street.

A BIRTHDAY

I never felt so much
Since I have felt at all
The tingling smell and touch
Of dogrose and sweet briar,
Nettles against the wall,
All sours and sweets that grow
Together or apart
In hedge or marsh or ditch.
I gather to my heart
Beast, insect, flower, earth, water, fire,
In absolute desire,
As fifty years ago.

Acceptance, gratitude:
The first look and the last
When all between has passed
Restore ingenuous good
That seeks no personal end,
Nor strives to mar or mend.
Before I touched the food
Sweetness ensnared my tongue;
Before I saw the wood
I loved each nook and bend,
The track going right and wrong;
Before I took the road
Direction ravished my soul.
Now that I can discern
It whole or almost whole,
Acceptance and gratitude
Like travellers return
And stand where first they stood.

ALL WE

All we who make
Things transitory and good
Cannot but take
When walking in a wood
Pleasure in everything
And the maker's solicitude,
Knowing the delicacy
Of bringing shape to birth.
To fashion the transitory
We gave and took the ring
And pledged ourselves to the earth.

IN LOVE FOR LONG

I've been in love for long
With what I cannot tell
And will contrive a song
For the intangible
That has no mould or shape,
From which there's no escape.

It is not even a name,
Yet is all constancy;
Tried or untried, the same,
It cannot part from me;
A breath, yet as still
As the established hill.

It is not any thing,
And yet all being is;
Being, being, being,
Its burden and its bliss.
How can I ever prove
What it is I love?

This happy happy love
Is sieged with crying sorrows,
Crushed beneath and above
Between to-days and morrows;
A little paradise
Held in the world's vice.

And there it is content
And careless as a child,
And in imprisonment
Flourishes sweet and wild;
In wrong, beyond wrong,
All the world's day long.

This love a moment known
For what I do not know
And in a moment gone
Is like the happy doe
That keeps its perfect laws
Between the tiger's paws
And vindicates its cause.